My First 500 Lovers

Trevor Church

napalm

Copyright © 2023 by Trevor Church

All rights reserved. Except as permitted under the U.S. Copyright Act of 1976, no part of this publication may be reproduced, distributed, or transmitted in any form or by any means, or stored in a database or retrieval system, without the prior written permission of the author.

napalm
Los Angeles, CA
IG: TrevorFawcettMajors
www.TrevorChurch.com
Originally published in paperback by napalm.
FIRST TRADE EDITION: APRIL 2023
The Library of Congress has cataloged the paperback edition as follows:
Church, Trevor
My First 500 Lovers /
Trevor Church. – 1st ed.
ISBN: 979-8-218-19161-0

1. Nonfiction – Poetry – LGBT. 2. Nonfiction – Biography & Autobiography – LGBT. 3. Nonfiction – Memoir 4. Nonfiction – Sex and Relationships

To #77, #80, and #163 for the
lessons you taught me

"Cold was the steel of my axe to grind
For the boys who broke my heart"

Taylor Swift

"When we look into our own hearts and begin to discover what is confused and what is brilliant, what is bitter and what is sweet, it isn't just ourselves that we're discovering. We're discovering the universe."

Pema Chödrön

"There are some things I know for certain: always throw spilled salt over your left shoulder, keep rosemary by your garden gate, plant lavender for luck, and fall in love whenever you can."

Practical Magic

There's a time in your youth when you aren't scared of anything - it's a time before falling is associated with pain and jumping in the deep end is exhilarating and blue instead of cold and lifeless. As you get older, fear changes from new wisdom and associations. By puberty I no longer feared the dark, but developed fears around sex: who was I even interested in? How do you do it? What if I'm bad? What if I climax too quickly? After a healthy dose of awkward teen sex, the fears changed again. Was I impure? Was I dirty? Should I feel shame?

I began documenting my relationships in Polaroids and notes in my journals. I don't know my actual "number." Between 1 and 2,000 my fears and insecurities and confidence have moved as unpredictably as a tornado.

There have been times I was ashamed of the sex I've

had and my body. There have been times where sex was a power move - a tool. There have been times when it was for sport, times when it was for guilt, times when it was for the chase, times when it was out of fear, boredom, or for distraction and times when it was for love.

    I don't always know much about the people I've been with, but through them I've learned a great deal about myself. These are the 500 I thank, for better or worse, for showing me things I hadn't seen.

1. I was 13. He was twice my age and a musician. It obviously was a secret.

2. I was 14, he was thirty. We would meet up at the playground of my old elementary school. We met in a chatroom.

3. I was 14, he was twice
that. Another musician. A type
was developing. Fuck you and
your Grammy. I was just a kid.

4-8. I had a type
But I was also a type
For some men
It was exciting at the time
Thinking love was being
Out of control
The secrets were exhilarating
Russel, David, Danny, Michael,
Anthony.
Now that I'm their age
It's not exhilarating
It keeps me up at night
It's Shigella
Bloodying my gut
Maiming my mind

9. We were a secret throughout high school and college. I was a secret to all of our friends and your family. The only secret I kept from you was that I loved you and still do.

10. You were a security guard at a department store. Another adult. You said you liked me. I thought it was true. We had sex in the mall parking lot on your lunch break.

11. You were a freshman in college. It was a secret. I would drive 30 minutes, pick you up, and take you home later. This went on for two years. A decade later when I ran into you, I found out I didn't even know your real name. Joe, Jason, Caleb.

12. You were my friend's prom date from another school. We had a time when everyone else fell asleep in the hotel that night.

13. I met him at an AA
meeting. He was a lawyer in
Ft. Lauderdale. He would
always tell me I was immature.
I was - I was a child.

14. Once I asked him why he always drives in the right lane on the highway
"I don't like competition."

\

15. I cared about Stephano a lot
Or the idea of him at least
I can't separate people from the idea of us sometimes

16. Frank had all gold teeth
And neck tattoos
He was everything I've ever wanted physically

17. Tomas stayed uninvited
I didn't want to have sex
The shower was broken
We smelled
I did it anyway

18. Dale was scared of commitment
That's something I can sympathize with
I wasn't scared though

19. Connor wasn't a dog person
I wasn't a Connor person

20-22. I dated two men named Travis
They both killed themselves
I dated a guy named Jake too
He shot himself
(not in chronological order)

23. Ismael ghosted me
physically
But kept texting me

24. Ivan texted me his number after we went home together
And then never talked to me again

25. Jared wanted like five
kids
My hips aren't great
For childbearing

26. I could've just bought
Kevin a portable charger
His phone was always dead
Because he was addicted to
Pokemon Go
It annoyed me

27. I need to stop dating
people named Trevor
It just gets weird every time

28. I made fun of Doug publicly for getting a DUI. That wasn't cool. That's how I flirted at nineteen. We got tattoos together at 2am. It ended when you got mad I wanted time with my friends.

29. I dated a man named Todd
He would listen to police
scanners while we fucked
In the parking lot across from
Voodoo Doughnut in Portland
After the ninth shooting
I called it quits

30. I dated a man named Dan
He was in love with me
Eight years later and he still
calls crying

31. Chet said he had an
autoimmune disease
He never said which
He was always sick
I felt bad, and do, but I
wanted adventure

32. You are the only man I've ever introduced to my family. I was shitty to you and still stalk your Instagram in secret.

33. Brandon said he wanted a boyfriend
He just wanted sex
Maybe I did too

I always liked them bad, and still do. He was the worst - a Portland Ted Bundy on a bicycle, slinging vegan pizza, chugging pbr, and choosing violence whenever he drank tequila. But this isn't that story. You've heard the stories of these men, holding you underwater in the tub, throwing you through a door, fingerprints on your throat. And losing my security deposit from all of those things. It's about how he read me poetry in bed until I fell asleep. Bad guys do sweet things sometimes. I didn't identify with Stockholm Syndrome ever: it's not developing positive feelings for abusers over time. It's already having positive feelings and it turning ugly. The sweet things they can do… it's the juxtaposition that keeps you. The worse they are, the greater the small deeds seem. As I later hypothesize here, it's addiction. Love is a

chemical imbalance. Good or
bad, it's all a mental
illness. And like any
addiction, you keep going back
after the bad because the good
is just so damn good. Or you
think it is at least. At the
time.

34. Troy never wore deodorant
And had the worst BO
He was gorgeous,
But I couldn't let it slide

35. I nagged Devon for no reason
Nonstop
I was incessant

36. Anthony was hard to read
And I don't like having to
guess emotions
I'm annoying like that

37. I was nineteen when I met Nate.
He was in the army, and almost twice my age.
I wanted a relationship - he led me on.
This was on and off for years. He lost interest when I turned 21.
He taught me sex isn't always fair or even for both parties, can hurt, and sometimes men take advantage of an ingenue.

38. Owen? I dated him too
He liked when strangers would
watch us

39. I dated a man named Dave
He didn't like being watched
by me or anyone

40. Craig - now a missing person

41. I dated Tom
Tom was sweet, even after he hit me
Or pushed me over a table at flip in Bloomingdales

42. Steve was funny and
thought I was funny
When I asked him to delete the
nude photos of me
He posted on his Tumblr
And Twitter

43. Noel was a politician
We watched the news
Three times a day

44. Spencer took my heart
He fed it to a Doberman

45. Mason jar memories
E minor chords
Orange creamsicle push pops
Are these things the time
capsule of us?

46. Shamus was from Ireland
Go figure
Most stereotypical name ever
His addiction to Adderall kept me up all night
I need my beauty sleep

47. Colton wanted to stay in
When I wanted to go out
When I wanted to stay in
He wanted to go out
Different wavelengths

48. Steve was when I tried dating nice
I got bored
He did nothing wrong - ever
Which is great for a sane person

49. I would get weirdly
jealous with Andre
It's not a normal
characteristic of mine
I was too toxic and needed to
work on myself

50. Tyler wanted open only
I wanted monogamous only
Neither was willing to
compromise

51. I thought Miguel and I hit it off
When the power went out in Texas
When the winter storm passed
So did he
I was left with nothing but the flu

52. Kevin was a dick
And not like the emotionally
unavailable kind I like
He was just a dick

53. Brandon would leave dishes
until they grew mold
I could never bring myself to
eat off his dishes
Even after they were clean
I just continued to see the
mold that had been on them
I already have issues around
eating

54. Jared loved jokes
He made them constantly
It was sweet
I was not

55. Archie hated music and movies
I love books too, but I need more
Kafka could only take us so far

56. Darren would drive us through the snow
Listening to Judy Garland
That's all we ever would do though

57. Alex had a drug problem
Alex said he was rushing to
the airport to find me in the
security line
Before my flight to New
Zealand
To kiss me, and say he would
wait for me
He didn't make it before
takeoff
His drug dealer had called

58. Antwon wanted to come back
from Germany with me
I didn't enjoy sex with him

59. Nick said "can't we just be friends?"
No, we can't

60. Andrew didn't tip well,
and was rude to servers
I used to be a server
No tolerance for that shit

61. I never forgave Jesse
For the Shigella infection
He gave me

62. David and I had another date scheduled
He hadn't realized it was for Super Bowl Sunday
I refused to reschedule
He refused to come
Wasn't my finest moment

63. Cory didn't like cuddling
I thought I could deal
When it grew cold
We grew cold - so did I

64. Leighton said he was asexual
I said that was fine
I lied to myself, and said he would get over it
That's not how sexuality works
I know better

65. I dated a girl once
She's in jail
She stabbed someone

66. Michael wanted to call me
nick in bed
I obliged
He did his thing while I
watched tv

67. Nick had a diaper fetish
And was from Kansas
I wanted to understand, but
Kansas just isn't my thing

68. I was gonna marry Andrew
And his money
And his career
But I look bad in khaki

69. I dumped you for no real reason other than interest in another man as I dropped you off at work. Not my finest moment. I've made sure to be more respectful to other men.

70. Another man had a mother with one leg. This was his only real talking point. He stole my Cherie Currie memoir and I didn't hear from him again.

71. Dante cried in bed

72. Peter slept with his eyes open
That's not a metaphor

73. Todd was a fucker
74. Kyle wasn't
But Kyle brought me to meet
his mom on our third date

75. Jason ate salad with his hands
In fancy restaurants
He said he was anti-capitalism
I didn't follow the correlation

76. You had a micro penis and a big crush on me. We slept together in your dorm room at a Christian university. You were the first person I ever ghosted, and when I saw you in passing months later, I saw how badly I could hurt someone.

77. We were never lovers
physically, but I loved you.
I still do.
Our morning walks around
Portland.
Our evening walks slicing the
skyline like the avocado you
eat on toast.
A part of my heart lives at
the top of Mt. Tabor –
-The part that never stops
beating.
"And I wake with your memory
over me
That's a real fucking legacy
to leave."

78. I found a way to stay in touch with you while I was in Cuba - finding a method of correspondence around no cell phone service, and no public internet. You fucked my roommate while I was scribbling postcards on the beach, like a fucking horse girl. Never be a horse girl.

79. Nevin showed me around Sacramento. We slept together. The following day at the Kamala rally, I turned around and he was holding someone else's hand.

80. You loved me with your whole heart, and I stabbed it and watched you bleed all the way back to Wisconsin. I hope time really heals all wounds. It kills me I hurt you.

81. I broke up with you on bleaker street for a boy in Brooklyn.

82. The boy in Brooklyn dumped me in Queens for a girl in Long Island. And I still think of you when anyone mentions that drink, Amy Fisher, or Lindsay Lohan.

83. Blake lived in my dad's old house in Portland when we met.
We slept together on and off for ten years.
I ran into him in Minnesota once, his mom lived next door to my mom.
Despite the synchronicity, it wasn't love.
It would've been in a movie.

84. Josh "J" took me out for my birthday, gave me a great day, made me fall hard for him, and then ghosted me, came back, and ghosted me again, and then a third time just to put salt in the wound while I was writing this. It wrecked me. He was one of the worst. A pathological psycho who still frightens me

85. Andrew dumped me on my birthday after we had sex.

86. Stefan also slept with me on my birthday, said we would go out to dinner - nine years later and I'm still waiting by the phone. I've stopped making love on my birthday - birthday sex doesn't end well for me.

87. I was impatient, unkind, and needy. You had never dated a man, or had sex with one. You promised you were gay, and then you left me for a girl.

88. You had divorced my friend – a woman – years earlier. We slept together after a party at her house that night. We spent the whole time laughing, hoping your kids and she wouldn't wake up. You made me pee out the window so I didn't open the door, and tickled me when I did. You were the first person to show me you could laugh during sex – you could be fun, funny, and sexy. It didn't have to be all business. I expected more drama from the incident, but everyone thought it was funny. We came close, but never slept together again. I understand, and still cherish you showing me laughter.

89. Like everyone I sleep with, I listened to the Rolling Stones while we were going at it. For awhile, I associated them with you, but they were mine. It took a moment, but I realized Mick Jagger would want me to have them more than you. I reclaimed them. I hope you think of me every time you hear them.

90. You were the second and last married man I slept with. You are married to a friend. It didn't ruin your marriage but ruined the friendship. I miss the friendship, but I'm ashamed to say I miss you more. I don't know if it's real or wanting what I can't have.

91. After you left, I had to tap my chest and ask "is this thing still on?"

92. On the day of the naked bike ride, I blew your phone up. I kept blowing it up. It annoyed you and you left. I knew I was acting crazy, but I still wanted to blame you.

93. Patrick, I thought it was love, you told me it was an experiment.

94. I lied to you, was on drugs, needy, impossible, and not understanding. I cheated on you and then accused you of doing it, and you dumped me.

95. You were much younger than me. I tried to do everything right: be ethical, tell him my intentions and feelings, don't mislead, he's young - don't break his heart. He ghosted me. We also had the same name - that's a weird thing that can happen when you're gay.

96. The next younger person I dated also ghosted me.

97. Ethan
98. Nathan
Internalized homophobia
(Not in chronological order)

99. There was also Jesse, who met my friends on my birthday. He kept saying he could never date a man - although he did immediately after me. I was crazy, and not on meds, and he was a violent alcoholic. The sick truth is, I would have let him beat the shit out of me again and again if he had just stayed. A black eye fades but my insecurities and loneliness feel forever.

100. I wanted a reason to talk to you, so I said the mole on the back of your neck looked cancerous and you should see a doctor. It didn't. But you talked to me. It didn't work out. Relationships based on cancerous lies never work.

101. Arthur showed me around Mexico.
I would've followed his tattooed body and snake bites through cartel run jungles.
He talked all night about wanting to visit me.
And then he ghosted me.

102. Enrique was quiet, probably because there was a language barrier.
Despite this we kept coming back to each other. Moving across Quintana like magnet and steel and all that cheesy crap.

103. Kyle was a white rapper. He slept with me and then my neighbor - right after. And got upset when I kicked him out for it.

Frat boys I just couldn't bro out with:

104. Nolan
105. Peter
106. Steve
107. Miko
(Not in chronological order)

108. Ben was a straight neighbor.
We never slept together when we were neighbors, but the second I moved, it happened. He won't even follow me back on Instagram now.

109. Ramiro would be sweet in bed and then just before the climax, he would physically hurt me, every time, so I could never finish. And he would get mad that I didn't like the pain. At this point in my life I'd finally gained enough confidence to say "get out." Ten years ago, I would've been black and blue.

110. Phillipe left me bloody, literally. With scratch marks and bites and bruises. I was in pain for a week, but felt obligated to let him continue. I wasn't comfortable saying stop.

111. Sam and I had sex.
Sam said he liked me.
Sam ghosted me.
Sam got wifeyed up during the pandemic.
Sam asked for a threesome.
I was talking to his partner who said I was being too forward for them being strangers.
Sam never told his partner we had a past.
Sam said I was a stranger.
Maybe I am? Does sex equal acquaintances?

112. Another Sam I really liked.
We hooked up under the noses of our friends.
He kept it a secret.
I wanted more.
He didn't.
Then he hooked up with a leprechaun.
I'd be lying if I didn't say it hurt my ego.

113. Another Sam.
This time in Playa Del Carmen.
We had a great day, and night.
He said he would see me
Thursday.
Thursday at 9 he said he
wasn't coming.
It doesn't matter what country
you're in, men are men.

114. Albert is getting a fake name in this book because he is still in the closet. He had a secret thing with a friend during college and slept with me after. He then went on to marry a woman. His dad broke his jaw and nose once. This is why he will probably stay married to a woman until he dies.

115. And he might tell you over a text.
And you might run along the waterfront.
And you might have Robyn and Sinead blaring in your headphones.
And you might watch the night sky unfold over the river.
And you might write another poem about it to add to your book of poems about it.
And you might win another award for it and cash in bigger royalty checks because of it.
And you might make sure that poetry collection is sold at his bookstore.
And you might make him question everything every time another customer walks out with it.
And you might take a Valium at night to forget about it.
And you might invite another man over to distract you from it.

And you might fill your face
with more plastic because if
it.
And you might, and you will,
and you ought to, because it's
all you've ever known.

116. Kenny was a straight boy
I went to college with.
I liked Kenny's brother but
slept with Kenny anyway - kind
of. He had the largest penis
I've ever seen in my life.
There wasn't much we could do.

117. Taylor was just a dick to everyone
And so cynical
He made me discover my own optimism

118. Matteo showed me around Berlin.
We danced all night to the Grease soundtrack at a lesbian bar.
Things ended when we got in an argument over Italian guards having large rifles just standing around Rome: you were in favor, I was against.

119. Eduardo showed me Rome and sang Katy Perry's "Fireworks" to me on the canals. We ate bread under a bridge in the middle of the night, and had sex over the crumbs, by some rats.

120. Sven and I first had sex at a Rolling Stones concert in Prague, and then again at his place. He spoke no English and I no Czech. We waved goodbye after frustrations over communication.

121. Grant was a drunk, a drug addict, and worked in a lab. He planned on becoming a doctor (maybe he did?). We met Eileen Myles together. She told you to stay warm in the winter, and then went on to say heartfelt things to me. You were upset she wrote you off and engaged with me. It became a crack in a foundation where I was blamed for everything.

122. Mac was my crutch on and off for years. I wanted to like you as more than friends. The magic we found in that abandoned house during the rainstorm dwindled, and we became just friends.

123. Arturo had been married twice, and I would've been a third for a green card if he'd wanted. I liked him a lot - even the weird patches of hair on his back. He dumped me because I didn't want to spend money to go on a yacht party.

124. Aaron was special and kind and awkward and fun, but kissed with his teeth and I couldn't handle it anymore. I still regret not just telling you. Now that I'm older, I'm more open about things that bother me.

125. I called you Queen. You were an Israeli living in Germany. We explored the ruins of the Berlin Wall together. I thought "let's fight fascism and fuck." I still have fantasies about someone saying that to me before stripping. I left you at a train stop in Munich.

126. Eric.
Data N/A.

Others with no data:
127. Cage
128. Jorge
129. Fernando
130. Matt
131. Johnny
132. Sam
133. Taylor
134. Riley
135. Kyle
136. Raul
137. Alexander
138. Brian
139. Bryan
140. Stephen
141. Darnell
142. Sacha
143. Amir
144. Aman
145. Nick
146. Curtis
147. Tom
148. Leonard
149. Ben
150. Randy
151. Chris
(Not in chronological order)

152. I was the other woman who believed every word. You even called me "kid" and left me a heartbroken cliche on the side of Santa Monica Blvd.

153. I met Blake when he was on tour. The affair went from Portland to San Diego. When we left the bar in Hillcrest that day, before the squirrel peed in my eye, the bartender said "be careful with him." I dumped you in the parking lot of a Church's chicken because I didn't want to compete with benzos and opiates - I'm always competing with them. I always thought we would get back together, but you started watching Fox news. Just another polo-wearing laguna beach republican now.

154. Paul was older but sweet.
He had no flaws.
I liked him.
But he's older, and I have a
fear of dating someone older,
because they might die first,
and then I'm alone again.
It's irrational but I always
think about it.

155. We met when we were both single but never met up before I left town. When I came back, you were married but it was an open marriage. I knew you liked me more, and if I had said "let's run off" you would've, but you'd already said I do, so therefor I don't.

156. You worked in the convenient store below me. After we finally had sex, you ghosted me. Months later I saw you, you said I looked like I gained weight.

157. You were a regular at the convenient store below me. You showed me Oingo Boingo. We talked all night after we had sex. I thought "maybe he'll stay." You thought "maybe not."

158. You were Brazilian and perfect aesthetically. But you dry humped my naked body aggressively while watching Ocean's Twelve - for the entire 2.5 hour movie.

159. Jimmy was a Brit living in New Zealand. I met him in Takaka. We were working on a farm together. He had a partner a few miles down the road, but they were open. We would lay in the middle of a field late at night, smoking rolled cigarettes, talking about our hopes. I knew I loved you when we went skinny dipping in Golden Bay. I never told you.

160. I met George sunbathing in Wellington. His parents had a mansion overlooking the city. We went there to have sex and eat Dominos. We later had sex in a park midday, and went swimming again. I've tried to keep in touch but his bipolar has made it difficult.

161. We met at a club in Auckland
You told me Kiwi's had the longest foreskin
It was very long,
But I don't know if this is a fact

162. Your name sounded like "mother fucker." You'd just dumped the weatherman, and I really liked you, and not because you were on the Price is Right. I liked you because you were kind and normal. I was too different for you, and you called it quits.
"The price is WRONG, bitch!"

163. Jonathan was the perfect Texas cowboy right in Oregon by way of Austin. He had a cavity and I could smell it. I pushed him away because of this, and was horrible to him after. Years later, when I matured, I tried to get him back. He treated me as I'd treated him. I still feel sorry for the whole thing. And I treat people as I want to be treated now.

164. Spent all night in El Paso listening to your lies that were finally cut off by the sunrise

Had alcohol and/or drug problems:
165. Matt
166. Pierre
167. Aiden
168. Christopher
169. James
170. Bryan
171. Ricky
172. Michael
173. Joel
174. Fahad
175. Jacob
176. Tyler
177. Jesse
178. Adelso
179. Jose
180. Steve
181. Russell
182. Pedro
183. Glen
(Not in chronological order)

184. Carlos
You were rude to waiters, hosts, and doormen. I refuse to apologize on your behalf.

185. You came on strong at a time that was bad for me. It took me all day, but I got the courage to tell you the truth. "Just friends."

186. You're an ex cop from New Braunfels, Texas. It never would've worked but it still stung when it didn't. Even when I found out you voted for Trump

187. You were the perfect man, but only visiting Austin from Atlanta. That's just how it goes.

188. I would've followed you off a cliff like you were some 2022 prophet.

189. Aaron
190. Mike
191. John
192. Carl
193. Dimitry
194. Cameron
195. Chris
Nothing to report

196. You came over after we met at the Orville Peck concert, because how could we not after his voice warmed the night air in that bumfuck Texas town?

197. "Hey cowboy, let's get out of here?"
"And do what?"
"I'm gonna teach you to ride a bull."

198. Peter was cruel
And horribly abusive
I saw him at Target once after
He was with a guy
When he walked away for a second
I approached the guy
And said "be careful with him."

199. Those creamy white thighs
Those ineffable eyes
Won't you take me home with you
And you did
For a moment

200. Andrew was perfect in
every single way
I really thought he liked me
Because he said he did
Why do they say that?
I'm a slut - they don't need
to.

201. Giancarlo was unemployed and lived on a cot in a room with someone else
I still was crazy about him
Until during pillow talk he discussed astral projecting with a cat
Something he does when he is bored

202. Josh seemed exciting.
He directed music videos
In Portland, that's about as
famous of a director as you'll
find
But he was violent and cruel

203. Tristan was great the first time we went to bed
The second time he couldn't get hard and said it was me

204. Jason and Clark were a couple
We would all meet up
One time Jason and I met up alone
He said "I can't do this to Clark" and left
He texted me saying "you were more attractive a couple of months ago."

205. I can't remember your name
I have a polaroid of you
I can remember your smegma,
and how it smelled the second
you took off your pants
I vomited

206. There's an epidemic of
meth use in the gay community
I have ignored it frequently
with partners, but don't
partake
I ignored it with you
But couldn't when I found out
you had a kid in the next room
I also slept with your
roommate (207)

208. Cesar was young but I was smitten
You said you hadn't experienced enough life yet
And you hadn't, I don't blame you.

209. I slept with an unmarried republican congressman once
He loved baseball and hated Roe V Wade
I was always tempted to write about him to get him voted out
But he lost his seat a few years after he lost me

210. I met Jesus through
Pachito
Pachito played guitar outside
7-Eleven
Jesus was his nephew
Jesus was 18
I was 21
I liked Jesus
Jesus liked an experiment

211. The second politician I slept with, Jim, was on city council
He wanted me to run his campaign
I said yes, and then discovered from the newspaper that he hired someone else
He would call me his "little monkey."
Men lie a lot, politicians lie more, male politicians? Forget about it.

212. Nigel was kind and hot, with good taste.
He lived with his mother, had no job, and got addicted to heroin
I always want to google him, knowing there's no way he's still alive
But I also don't want the evidence

213. Josh was straight
He told me it was just sex
I knew it was just sex
Knowing that doesn't stop me
from getting attached always

Other straight male
experiments:
214. Ken
215. Brad
216. Austin
217. Eric
218. Matt
219. Gabriel
220. Ren
221. Ruel
222. Karlitos
223. Matthew
224. Edgar
225. Matteo
226. Austen
227. Jordan
228. Colby
229. Tony
230. Alexander
231. Emilio
232. Isaiah
233. Vlad
(Not in chronological order)

234. Nate smelled like ramen
The chicken kind
I could only focus on food
around him

235. I stopped seeing you
because you smelled bad
Then I found videos you'd
posted on OnlyFans of us
Without my knowledge
I had to threaten you to take
them down.

236. I met Brandon through
Rose McGowan when I was seven
We have stayed in touch over
the years
And lived in Minneapolis at
the same time
Nothing concrete ever formed
though
And I'll never know why

237. I dated you and then I dated your ex.
I didn't like him but I did like you.
I gave you a sweater Travis, and years later I saw you in it.
I said "hey! I gave you that sweater!"
You said "cool" and walked away.
I'd thought we ended on good terms.
Interestingly your ex was my friend's older brother
Who I'd had a crush on when I was little

238. Riley was nice but wanted me to settle down
Not settle down as in marriage
But settle down as in cruises, and cargo shorts

239. Max was self-conscious about his body
Everything was lights off
No excessive touching
I tried to get in and touch his soul
I never got there

240. I write to remember and I write to forget
A bad tattoo
Remember a love and remember that we once cared but forget the pain when we stopped caring

241. Tanner was my friend's brother
He was younger
And didn't know what he wanted

Right guy (maybe) wrong time (definitely):
242. Andy
243. Edward
244. Rory
245. Nicholas
246. Christ
247. Colter
248. Billy
249. Evan
250. Bennett
251. Cody
252. Harry
253. Brian
254. Christian
255. Grayson
256. Haley
257. Adan
258. Lou
259. Lewis
260. Nathaniel
261. Jeremy
262. Miguel
263. Blake
(Not in chronological order)

264. I wanted it so bad it
killed me
It still kills me
I want, I want, I want
Everyone says I want too much

265. I dated a pornstar
266. And his boyfriend
He was plagued by a traumatic southern childhood
And the gay plague
I hurt him, and he hurt me
His boyfriend got out unharmed
I think of him whenever I watch the Perks of Being a Wallflower

267. Christian was a tattoo artist who said I inspired his art
I liked him a lot
He stopped dating men and only dates women now

268. Another Christian wanted to fist me
I wasn't down for it
He said he couldn't be with someone who didn't do that

269. I knew Ted in high-school
We didn't connect until years later
We slept together for a moment
He kept saying he was straight
Eventually I found out he was using me to get to his ex girlfriend

270. You were the second and last pornstar I dated
I realized I'm too jealous to date someone in the industry

271. I hung around with you
and your partner for a bit
I liked you but wasn't into
him
So I had to say bye

272. Jackson had a scat fetish
It was never going to work out

273. Tony
274. Simon
275. Malcolm
Can't even remember
(not in chronological order)

276. Emiliano wanted to focus
on his career
I get it
That's what I'm doing now with
my bed and heart

277. Nico was proof
That loving Buffy isn't always enough
Not even Sarah Michelle Gellar could save us

278. I thought I hated Scott
for being opinionated
But I'm opinionated too
I just hated his opinions
Do opposites attract?
Or do we just tell ourself
that to settle?

279. Settling just means you're tired
I get it
I was tired with Andy for a moment

280. Garret ruined me
I thought we were in love
He dumped me in a bar
Because I didn't mind that
political parties can buy
mailing lists

281. Ian was my British bloke
Stereotypically dark and dry English humor
With thousands of miles and an ocean between
It never was gonna work
I still annoy him at 4am when space scares me
Or I want to commit suicide again
He never says 'poor thing' or offers pity
He remains real and unchanged

update Ian has died. Who will save my soul in the middle of the night?

282. One friend says I'm having a baby
Everything will change
One friend - the one I like, I see him
He ignores me
Everything has changed
And everyone's changing
And everything's changing
And I don't fit in here
And I don't fit in there
And I'm lonely
And I'll die alone
And I want someone

283. Terrence loved old movies
I loved talking to him about old movies
It was one of the best first dates I've ever had
He ghosted me
And then ghosted me again

284. Sex with Steve felt primordial
I cannot adequately explain
But that's all there was between us

We just weren't right for each other:
285. Trevor
286. Quincy
287. Santiago
288. Mitchell
289. Alejandro
290. Caleb
291. Adrian
292. Aldo
293. Rhyan
294. Joshua
295. Nicholas
296. Ali
297. Paul
298. Jake
299. Kyle
300. Drew
301. Martin
302. Glenn
303. Justin
304. George
(Not in chronological order)

305. You were quite a bit older
But I still liked you
You were my first guy in Austin
After we were together, you told me about him
Michel Rostand

306. I liked Trevor but there was a pandemic going on
I thought things were going great
And then he acted like it never happened
I still see him around socially in Portland

307. Hunter came on way too strong way too fast
I sort of regret ending it though

308. Devon and I met two days before I ended up in the hospital
He'd found someone by the time I was out
They're still together

309. I don't like farting
Like as a joke
I get that it's natural
But Pete would constantly do it
Like at me
Because he thinks flatulence is flirting?

310. Ryan was a drunk
Every single time we went out
He was drunk
I don't live like that

311. I ended up in the hospital while on my date with James
He came with
I didn't hear from him again
I met up with him again years later
And it just wasn't there

312. Paul was 6'9
Paul was sweet
Paul went "mmm mmm mmm"
nonstop, every single time we
were in bed
From start to finish

313. Aladdin was named after the Disney character he also looked like,
I liked him.
I got sick and we couldn't see each other for weeks,
I was also standoffish.
You met someone,
And I was unreasonably mad about it.
Maybe in another life.

314. You were a writer fresh out of prison
When we stood in the flooded streets of Baton Rouge
Donating goods
I thought I loved you

315. You were dying of a
neurological disorder
I kept thinking our story
would be a good book
That's not a good reason to
date someone

316. We sort of ghosted each
other Frank
I had nothing against you
I just didn't feel a spark
I guess you didn't either

317. Nolan lived in Santee, CA
I couldn't date someone who
lived all the way in Santee.

318. J lived way up in the hills outside of Riverside, CA.
I couldn't date someone who lived all the way in the hills.

319. Seth told me I came on too strong
Then texted me again
I said I didn't think it would work
He got mad at me for not giving another chance

320. James I thought was great
James never called me back
James still watches my
Instagram stories
James knows this book is
coming out
James, are you reading this?

321. I liked Travis for his name, obviously
But he seemed so settled in his life
I didn't see myself fitting into it

322. Oleg
323. Logan
324. Ivan
(Not in chronological order)
All wanted polyamory
I want monogamy

325. Is all of this love shit just us trying not to die alone?
Because unless you're Thelma and Louise you die alone anyway
Is my compulsive need for romance just fear?
Compulsion is usually fear based

I was shitty to, and owe this public apology to:
326. Jay
327. Jonathan
328. Ben
329. Ethan
330. Jesse
331. Zack
332. Smarty
333. Sam
334. Alex
335. Jake
336. Adam
337. Patrick
338. Trevor
339. Tim
340. Daniel
(Not in chronological order)

341. Michael was patient with me
We started talking when I was very young
We didn't meet up until years later
When we did, he sat quietly while I flipped through his hundreds of copies of Time Magazine

342. Fernando ate my entire dinner
And then his came and he didn't offer me any
He never asked or offered to pay for it
He was mad when I said it wouldn't work

343. Daniel said he wasn't feeling it
And wasn't looking for anything serious
He could've told me before the date
But I don't resent him

344. Greg played on a gay football team
Greg and I watch Smile together
In it there are two men, Trevor and Greg
I thought our date went perfectly
He didn't

345. Fern
346. Tanner
347. Pete
They didn't make me laugh
(Not in chronological order)

348. Josh was addicted to meth
I tried to look past this
But he was too unreliable and
I ended it

349. I buried my face in my pillow
And said "I just want you to love me back"

350. Drew was the most arrogant man I've ever met I kept him around because I was so attracted to him

Nothing exciting to say
351. Derek
352. Nathan
353. Julio
354. Monty
355. Clay
356. Tate
357. Justin
358. Joseph
359. Michael
360. Alan
361. Keaton
362. Dean
363. Shawn
364. Cody
365. Carter
366. Rhett
367. Colin
368. Joey
369. Brandon
370. Everett
371. Liam
372. Oren
(Not in chronological order)

373. Sam requested that I wear
a jockstrap at all times
I requested that he hand feed
me pizza rolls at all times
We both had so many wants

374. Andy was my friend's little brother
I checked in on his feelings every step of the way
It just never became anything serious
Then he became a communist and it got weird

375. Matt was a brilliant writer
I wished I was half the writer he is
He never did anything with it though

376. Zach was one of the best
musicians I've ever met
We would write together
Our disorders kept us apart

377. Will was my best friend's protégé so to speak
Will said I wasn't fat enough for his taste

378. Brian threatened me when
I'd mentioned how we'd had sex
He said I couldn't say it out
loud
He dates women

379. CJ worked in television
He finally ended it when I
said I didn't care how much
money he made

380. Derek wanted to infect me
with his strain of HIV
He said it would bring us
closer
I said I don't believe in that
level of closeness

381. Your dad was a music producer
Your walls were lined with photos of you and Joni Mitchell, Keith Richards, Etc.
I wanted you,
You could tell it was mostly for your music connections

382. Charlie was a punk rocker
Decked out in a black flag
shirt
And a shaved head
He was a little older
It just fizzled out
He tasted like tea tree oil

383. Simon wanted more
More than I could give
I just couldn't

Not compatible in bed:
384. Logan
385. Jeff
386. Marshall
387. Cody
388. Bryce
389. Alfo
390. Stephen
391. Richie
392. Rod
393. Harrison
394. James
395. Rafael
396. Tristan
397. Ivan
398. Sam
399. Collin
400. Uriel
401. Kitan
402. Ari
403. Ryan
404. Nick
405. Edgar
406. Taylor
(Not in chronological order)

407. We both loved Jobriath
But you were a Bernie
And I was a Hillary

408. Jason
409. Bret
410. Hank
411. Connor
All nice but not right for me

412. You once told me:
"I like spending different types of time with you"
I still think it's my favorite thing anyone
Has ever said to me

413. Eric would say he didn't like me
And then call me again
I'd let him come over every time
My gut told me he was a serial killer
I asked him if he was
He never talked to me again

414. Jeb didn't like when I
made fun of his voice
I kept calling him Jeb Bush
I could have been nicer

415. Evan hated animals
I didn't know this until a few
dates in when he said
"I can't stand people who
bring their dogs places."
And then elaborated that it
wasn't just places, he just
couldn't stand dogs
Or cats

416. Jason was a republican
baseball player
He had rectal warts
I told him
Despite my reassurance, he
never talked to me again

417. Tyler was an Appalachian musician
I liked him a lot
He ghosted me
I gave him attention when he came back
He ghosted me again

418. Will said he was on his way
It was going to be our second date
He never showed up
And didn't respond to texts
Are you dead or just a dick?

419. Manuel wanted to marry me for a green card
I wanted to marry him for love
I was setting myself up for heartache

420. I was just mean to
Stephen for no reason
I couldn't control it
I don't know why and I'm sorry

421. Brad and I just wanted different things
It was a mutual agreement to split
We are still friends

422. Marshall didn't have a sense of humor
And hated when I called him Eminem
And when I offered him M&M's

423. Tate hated Courtney Love
I could never
She is the queen

424. I only dated Jasper
because I liked his name
It's a good fucking name

425. Dillon shared a name with my brother
No matter how hard I tried, I couldn't get over it

426. Cody shaved his back
So it was always prickly with stubble
Wax it, laser it, or leave it

427. Chris was a security guard at a friend's party
We had fun
But we just stopped texting eventually

428. Scott spent the night
counting stars with me
I wanted the sun to burn out
So the stars would've lasted
forever

429. I got clingy with Darnell
I always get clingy with the ones I want
They never want me back
The ones who want me?
I can't get far enough away from

Guys I got clingy with and scared off:
430. Grant
431. Greg
432. Thomas
433. Albert
434. Ryan
435. Nick
436. Taylor
437. Gerardo
438. Omar
439. Marc
440. Warren
441. Cesar
442. Luis
443. Daniel
444. Leo
445. Kyle
446. Axel
447. Thiago
448. Christopher
(Not in chronological order)

449. No, voting for Jill Stein
wasn't a good fucking idea
Neither was going on a date
with you
The supreme court thanks you
I do not

Other Guys I broke up with
because of politics:
450. Stephen
451. Ben
452. Anthony
453. Nic
454. Spencer
455. JD
456. Beau
457. Hugo
458. David
459. Stiven
460. Roman
461. John
462. Peter
463. Kaleb
464. Will
465. Jay
466. Arturo
467. Brent
468. Oscar
469. Keaton
(Not in chronological order)

470. I'm sorry I tried to hold your hand
I'm sorry I tried to hold your heart
I'm sorry I tried to hold my space

471. Josh was my neighbor
Another neighbor
I still haven't learned my lesson
It's never good when the person you're dating
Can see through your window

472. Chase liked me because I write
Chase doesn't like that I'm writing about him now
You can't have it both ways

473. Zach
474. Zack
475. Zac
476. Zachary
Different spellings for the same mistake
(Not in chronological order)

477. I wanted to just make it
to the point where
We say I love you
Because I wanted to hear you
say the word love
Didn't happen

478. Preston wasn't attracted to me physically
I can't change that
I get that it's shallow and I get that sometimes
We can't help it

479. Jake kept calling me a democratic whore
Why would I have stayed with you?

480. Jackson didn't believe in vaccines
Or taxes
And I can't love someone stupid

481. Chris played me
And played me
And played me
I can still hear the orchestra

482. Carter was bipolar
He couldn't keep it under control
And kept me awake
For weeks at a time

483. I was told it would
change when I got older
When my prefrontal lobe was
fully formed
But I'm older and it's formed
And I'm still here
Doing the same shit
With the same results
And the same feeling
In my gut
In my head
In my heart
Did I not grow up?
Do any of us ever?
Or is it something we're all
just faking
A false reality
Am I Keanu?
Hello matrix, it's me.

484. Sampson said I tried too hard
If changing his name to Samson
And singing Regina Spektor is trying too hard
Then I can't change

485. I went back and forth with Ben
I love you, I love you not
He got tired of my antics

486. Bennett looked like Harry Potter
He even had a birthmark on his head that reminded one of Harry's scar
He was perfect on paper
And maybe in actuality
I'm not actually sure why it dimmed

487. Christian was born on the same day Kennedy died, in the same city Kennedy died in. He also worked in politics. I'm not sure if he had anything in common with JFK, but the things he told me held as much weight as Kennedy conspiracy theories. I think maybe the conspiracy theories hold even more. He ruined my first few months in Austin. He said he'd call me in a month to reconnect. It never came. He is one of the only 500 I regard as a mistake. I believed every fucking word.

488. One could argue love is a mental illness
It messes with your dopamine and serotonin
Like bipolar, depression, and drug abuse
You can be addicted to love
Like drugs
Love can make you soar like mania
And bell bottom blues bury you like manic depression
These things - bipolar, depression, addiction. They're illnesses that are diagnosable and treatable.
Should the DSM identify love as another disorder so someone will try to fucking cure us of it?
And should we be cured of it like those diseases and other disorders? And would you want to be? At times I've wanted to be but maybe that's just me in my moments of anguish.
A life without love like that isn't terrible. There's family, friends, and fun times. What I'm saying is, I'd

love necessary? And should I
seek treatment?

There are elven names I cannot
remember, despite having
polaroids of these gentlemen.
I did not write their name in
my journals or on the photos
for some reason.

500. We hit it off right away.
You were into me, I could
tell.
We hung at Fraziers. I ate
corndogs, you drank.
I said I wanted to hang again,
You said "I really want to.
Saturday?"
Saturday came and you never
showed.

It's been difficult writing this because I hate men. I am a cis man, who identifies as a man, who is only attracted to men. Men define my life, and unfortunately that won't change. Everything I love about myself is a confidence a man has given me, and everything I hate about myself is a scar a man has left me. Having to go back and examine 500 different men I've been intimate with has made me repulsed at times, and more forgiving at other times. I often say "I hate men," but it's complicated. I hate the default, I hate the power, I hate the misogyny and sexism and internalized homophobia held by men who say things like "masc men only." I hate the self-hating gays, and at times I hate myself (but not for being gay). I can't say definitively if my views on men have changed after writing this, but it's something I hope to understand before I make it through the next 500.

I was hoping to end this book on a high note, but this is nonfiction and Prince Charming doesn't always show up on time. If there is such a thing as a soulmate, I haven't found him yet. But I continue to seek out this feeling I've only found a handful of times. It's a feeling of nausea, and like your colon is falling through your asshole. It's a moment of nervousness at a hand touch followed by a warm rush only comparable to heroin. It's that kiss that every band ever has written a song about. The one that knocks you on your ass and feels airtight. It's more than that. It's soul-tight. It's what all the kids call love. And you spend forever chasing that feeling or give up in demolished despair. And that chase? It's addiction. That's why they call heroin addiction

chasing the dragon. And maybe
it's vital. Maybe it's the
thing that keeps us going when
everything else is crashing
down. That chance to maybe
feel it again or feel it
forever. Maybe survival is
love. Or some hokey shit like
that. Maybe it's beautiful and
perfect and what we should
seek out and why we're here.
But if that's the case, too
many of us lose this game.
There's this guy on the West
Coast. He's the love of my
life, and everyone I meet, I
compare to him. I always will.
I will never find someone who
makes me feel the way he does.
Do I give in and give up? Or
do I keep fighting, hoping
somehow my brain will rewire
itself and give me this
feeling again with someone
else? Or maybe I should just
appreciate that I'm lucky
enough to have felt this way
once, and to have known what
it feels like to care so much
about someone you would put

their life before yours at any moment.

In writing this book, I connected with many of my old lovers. Some did not want to hear from me - fair. Others forgave me, and others I forgave. One particularly important one came to visit me at the completion of this book. I think I hoped the spark I'd initially felt would be there, but it wasn't. What was there is still important though: a friendship where we know each other in a special sort of way.

I think maybe looking for this rare connection makes the rest of the bullshit worth it. Maybe I'm wrong though, and all of this is a big fucking waste of time. Unfortunately, I'll have to wait until I'm on my deathbed to give a definitive answer on that.

Other Books by the Author

Anomie in America

Out of the Woods: The Witch Hunt & Hillary Clinton

The Gospel According to a Basket-Case

A History of Broken

The Day Portland Died: Three Generations of Murder

www.ingramcontent.com/pod-product-compliance
Lightning Source LLC
Chambersburg PA
CBHW070848050426
42453CB00012B/2085